U.S. Air Force Fighters

Carrie A. Braulick
AR B.L.: 3.2
Points: 0.5   MG

MILITARY VEHICLES

U.S.
AIR FORCE
FIGHTERS

by Carrie A. Braulick

Reading Consultant:
Barbara J. Fox
Reading Specialist
North Carolina State University

Capstone
press
Mankato, Minnesota

Blazers is published by Capstone Press,
151 Good Counsel Drive, P.O. Box 669, Mankato, Minnesota 56002.
www.capstonepress.com

Library of Congress Cataloging-in-Publication Data
Braulick, Carrie A., 1975–
    U.S. Air Force fighters / by Carrie A. Braulick.
    p. cm.—(Blazers. Military vehicles)
    Summary: "Provides an overview of the design, uses, weapons, and
equipment of U.S. Air Force fighter planes"—Provided by publisher.
    Includes bibliographical references and index.
    ISBN-13: 978-0-7368-5467-2 (hardcover)
    ISBN-10: 0-7368-5467-3 (hardcover)
1. Fighter planes—United States—Juvenile literature. 2. United States. Air
Force—Equipment and supplies—Juvenile literature. I. Title. II. Series.
UG1242.F5B734 2006
623.74'64'0973—dc22   2005016443

Editorial Credits
Jenny Marks, editor; Thomas Emery, designer; Jo Miller, photo researcher/
    photo editor

Photo Credits
Digital Vision, 17
DVIC/Blake R. Borsic, 6; Master Sgt. Lochner, 19 (bottom); SR. Airman
    Theodore J. Koniares, 19 (top); SRA James Harper, cover; Tech SGT
    Hans H. Dettner, 13
Getty Images Inc./David McNew, 27
Lockheed Martin Aeronautics Company, 26
Photo by Ted Carlson/Fotodynamics, 5, 9, 11, 12, 15 (both), 20, 25,
    28–29
Photo by U.S. Air Force/AFFTC History Office, 22–23; Staff Sgt.
    Derick C. Goode, 10; Staff Sgt. Jeffery A. Wolfe, 21; Tech. Sgt.
    Debbie Hernandez, 7

**Capstone Press thanks Raymond L. Puffer, PhD, Historian, Air
Force Flight Test Center, Edwards Air Force Base, California for his
assistance in preparing this book.**

1 2 3 4 5 6 11 10 09 08 07 06

TABLE OF CONTENTS

Air Force Fighters

Enemies do not want to face a U.S. Air Force fighter plane. A fighter can quickly turn a target into a heap of burning rubble.

The U.S. Air Force has the best fighter planes in the world. These planes are fast, and their aim is deadly.

BLAZER FACT

The F-15 Eagle has a
perfect combat record.
No F-15 has ever been
shot down in battle.

DESIGN

Fighters are built to blast enemy planes out of the sky. They **protect** soldiers on the ground too. Some fighters also bomb land targets.

A-10 THUNDERBOLT IIs

Large engines push fighters to high speeds. The F-15 Eagle is the fastest fighter in the world. It flies 1,875 miles (3,017 kilometers) per hour.

REAR OF F-15 ENGINES

F-15 EAGLES

BLAZER FACT

Most Air Force fighters can fly faster than the speed of sound.

F-16 Fighting Falcons are powerful planes. Even at high speeds, they are easy to control. They make quick, sharp turns.

The F-117A Nighthawk was the first stealth fighter used by the U.S. Air Force. Its sleek shape keeps it from being spotted by enemy radar.

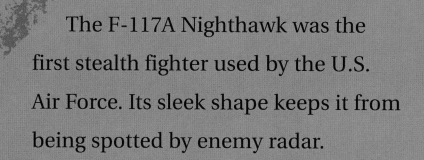

BLAZER FACT

Radar systems send out radar beams. Beams hit a plane and bounce back to show the plane's location.

WEAPONS AND EQUIPMENT

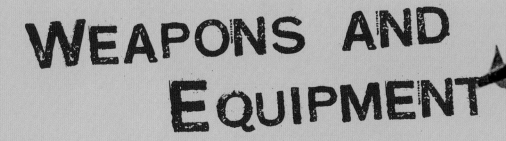

Fighters are packed with missiles and bombs. Fighters also fire bullets out of cannons.

Many fighters use guided missiles to destroy enemy planes. Sensors guide the weapons to their targets.

AIM-9 SIDEWINDER

AIM-9 SIDEWINDER

F-16 COCKPIT

Fighters have advanced electronic systems. Cockpit electronics help pilots steer the planes. Other systems protect the planes from enemy attacks.

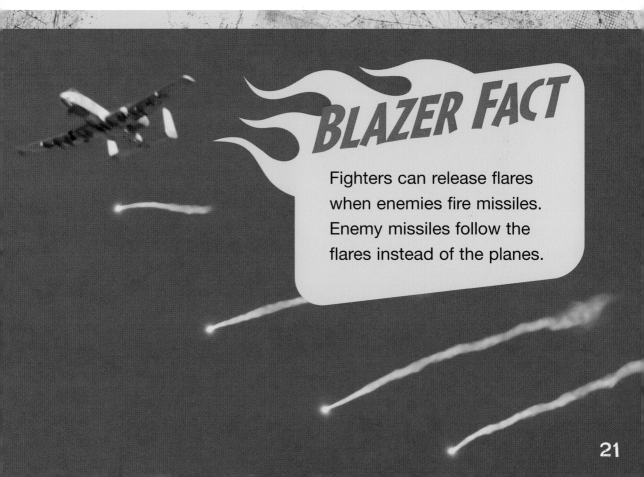

BLAZER FACT

Fighters can release flares when enemies fire missiles. Enemy missiles follow the flares instead of the planes.

F-16 FIGHTING FALCON

MISSILES

TAIL

AF 88 473

REAR OF ENGINE

MISSILE

COCKPIT

NOSE

FIGHTERS IN FLIGHT

Pilots wear oxygen masks and G suits. The masks help pilots breathe in thin air. G suits keep pilots safe when they make sharp turns at top speeds.

NIGHT VISION GOGGLES

OXYGEN MASK

G SUIT

PULL TO EJECT

The Air Force is always improving fighters. New and even more powerful planes will be used in the future. Enemies must beware of these fierce fighters!

F/A-22 RAPTOR

X-45 UNMANNED COMBAT AIR VEHICLE

BLAZER FACT

In the future, the Air Force may use unmanned fighters. Pilots will control these planes from the ground.

F-16s FLYING IN FORMATION!

GLOSSARY

bomb (BOM)—a container filled with explosives

bullet (BUL-it)—a small, pointed metal object fired from a gun

cannon (KAN-uhn)—a large gun

electronics (i-lek-TRON-iks)—products that run on small amounts of electricity

flare (FLAIR)—a bright object released by a fighter plane to make an enemy missile miss it

missile (MISS-uhl)—an explosive weapon that can fly long distances

radar system (RAY-dar SISS-tuhm)—equipment that uses radio waves to locate and guide objects

sensor (SEN-sur)—an instrument that detects physical changes in the environment

stealth fighter (STELTH FYE-tur)—a fighter plane designed to stay hidden from enemy radar

READ MORE

Holden, Henry M. *Air Force Aircraft.* Aircraft. Berkeley Heights, N.J.: Enslow, 2001.

Hopkins, Ellen. *U.S. Air Force Fighting Vehicles.* United States Armed Forces. Chicago: Heinemann, 2004.

Stone, Lynn M. *F-16 Fighting Falcon.* Fighting Forces in the Air. Vero Beach, Fla.: Rourke, 2005.

INTERNET SITES

FactHound offers a safe, fun way to find Internet sites related to this book. All of the sites on FactHound have been researched by our staff.

Here's how:

1. Visit *www.facthound.com*
2. Type in this special code **0736854673** for age-appropriate sites. Or enter a search word related to this book for a more general search.
3. Click on the **Fetch It** button.

FactHound will fetch the best sites for you!

INDEX